WORKING PAPERS

Financial Accounting

Chapters f1-f13

Eighth Edition

W. Steve Albrecht, PhD, CPA, CIA, CFE
Brigham Young University

James D. Stice, PhD
Brigham Young University

Earl K. Stice, PhD
Brigham Young University

K. Fred Skousen, PhD, CPA
Brigham Young University

SOUTH-WESTERN
THOMSON LEARNING™

Australia · Canada · Mexico · Singapore · Spain · United Kingdom · United States

Working Papers to accompany *Financial Accounting, 8e* by W. Steve Albrecht, James D. Stice, Earl K. Stice, and K. Fred Skousen

Publisher: Dave Shaut
Acquisitions Editor: Sharon Oblinger
Development Editor: Leslie Kauffman, Litten Editing and Production, Inc.
Production Editor: Kara ZumBahlen
Manufacturing Coordinator: Doug Wilke
Marketing Manager: Dan Silverburg
Promotions Manager: Jon Schneider
Production House: Jennifer Ballentine, Professional Book Center
Printer: Globus Printing

Printed in the United States of America
1 2 3 4 5 04 03 02 01

For more information contact South-Western, 5101 Madison Road, Cincinnati, Ohio, 45227 or find us on the Internet at http://www.swcollege.com

ISBN: 0-324-06763-1

Name ____________________

P2-5 Income Statement Preparation

P2-6 Expanded Accounting Equation

1.–5.

P2-7 Income Statement Preparation

1.

2.

P2-8 Statement of Cash Flows

1.

2.

Name ____________________

P2-9 Statement of Cash Flows

P2-10 Unifying Concepts: Net Income and Financial Ratio Analysis

1.

2.–4.

P2-11 Unifying Concepts: Net Income and Statement of Retained Earnings

1.

2.

P2-11 Concluded

3.

4.

P2-12 Financial Ratios

1.–2.

P2-13 Comprehensive Financial Statement Preparation

1.

P2-13 Continued

2.

P2-13 Concluded

3.–7.

Name ______________________________

P2-14 Elements of Comparative Financial Statements

1.–4.

P3-1 Journal Entries and Trial Balance

1.

P3-1 Continued

2.

Cash

Accounts Receivable

Inventory

Office Building

Accounts Payable

Mortgage Payable

Notes Payable

Capital Stock

Retained Earnings

Sales Revenue

Cost of Goods Sold

Salaries Expense

Utilities Expense

Interest Expense

P3-1 Concluded

2. Continued

3.

P3-2 Journalizing and Posting

1.

JOURNAL PAGE

	DATE	DESCRIPTION	POST REF.	DEBIT	CREDIT	
1						1
2						2
3						3
4						4
5						5
6						6
7						7
8						8
9						9
10						10
11						11
12						12
13						13
14						14
15						15
16						16
17						17
18						18
19						19
20						20
21						21
22						22
23						23
24						24
25						25
26						26
27						27
28						28
29						29
30						30
31						31
32						32

P3-2 Concluded

2.

Cash

Accounts Receivable

Inventory

Supplies

Accounts Payable

Capital Stock

Sales Revenue

Cost of Goods Sold

Insurance Expense

Utilities Expense

Wage Expense

3.

P3-3 Journal Entries from Ledger Analysis

1.

2.

Name ______________________________

P3-4 Journalizing and Posting Transactions

1.

JOURNAL

PAGE ______

	DATE	DESCRIPTION	POST REF.	DEBIT	CREDIT	
1						1
2						2
3						3
4						4
5						5
6						6
7						7
8						8
9						9
10						10
11						11
12						12
13						13
14						14
15						15
16						16
17						17
18						18
19						19
20						20
21						21
22						22
23						23
24						24
25						25
26						26
27						27
28						28
29						29
30						30
31						31
32						32

P3-4 Concluded

2.

Cash

Accounts Receivable

Equipment

Inventory

Accounts Payable

Cost of Goods Sold

Rent Expense

Utilities Expense

Salary Expense

Property Tax Expense

Sales Revenue

P3-5 Unifying Concepts: Compound Journal Entries, Posting, Trial Balance

1.

JOURNAL

PAGE

	DATE		DESCRIPTION	POST REF.	DEBIT	CREDIT	
1							1
2							2
3							3
4							4
5							5
6							6
7							7
8							8
9							9
10							10
11							11
12							12
13							13
14							14
15							15
16							16
17							17
18							18
19							19
20							20
21							21
22							22
23							23
24							24
25							25
26							26
27							27
28							28
29							29
30							30
31							31
32							32

P3-5 Continued

2.

Cash

Accounts Receivable

Inventory

Land

Building

Equipment

Office Equipment

Truck

Notes Payable

Capital Stock

Sales Revenue

Cost of Goods Sold

Interest Expense

P3-5 Concluded

3.

P3-6 Unifying Concepts: T-Accounts, Trial Balance, and Income Statement

1\.

ASSETS

Cash

Accounts Receivable

Notes Receivable

Inventory

Supplies

Land

Building

Equipment

LIABILITIES

Accounts Payable

Notes Payable

Mortgage Payable

OWNERS' EQUITY

Capital Stock

P3-6 Continued

1. Continued

RETAINED EARNINGS

Sales Revenue

Rent Revenue

Interest Revenue

Cost of Goods Sold

Wages Expense

Utilities Expense

Interest Expense

P3-6 Continued

2.

P3-6 Concluded

3.

P3-7 Transaction Analysis and Journal Entries

1.

JOURNAL PAGE

DATE	DESCRIPTION	POST REF.	DEBIT	CREDIT

P3-7 Continued

2.

JOURNAL

PAGE

	DATE		DESCRIPTION	POST REF.	DEBIT	CREDIT	
1							1
2							2
3							3
4							4
5							5
6							6
7							7
8							8
9							9
10							10
11							11
12							12
13							13
14							14
15							15
16							16
17							17
18							18
19							19
20							20
21							21
22							22
23							23
24							24
25							25
26							26
27							27

P3-7 Concluded

3.

Name ____

P3-8 Correcting a Trial Balance

P3-9 Unifying Concepts: Journal Entries, T-Accounts, Trial Balance

1.

JOURNAL

PAGE

	DATE	DESCRIPTION	POST REF.	DEBIT	CREDIT	
1						1
2						2
3						3
4						4
5						5
6						6
7						7
8						8
9						9
10						10
11						11
12						12
13						13
14						14
15						15
16						16
17						17
18						18
19						19
20						20
21						21
22						22
23						23
24						24
25						25
26						26
27						27
28						28
29						29
30						30
31						31
32						32

Name ______________________________

P3-9 Continued

2.

Cash

Notes Receivable

Accounts Receivable

Inventory

Land

Building

Furniture

Notes Payable

Accounts Payable

Capital Stock

Retained Earnings

Sales Revenue

P3-9 Concluded

2. Continued

Cost of Goods Sold	

Salary Expense	

Rent Expense	

3.

P4-3 Adjusting Entries

JOURNAL

PAGE

DATE		DESCRIPTION	POST REF.	DEBIT	CREDIT

P4-4 Year-End Analysis of Accounts

1.

2.

3.

P4-5 Year-End Analysis of Accounts

1.

2.

3.

P4-6 Account Classifications and Debit-Credit Relationships

Account Title	(1) B/S or I/S	(2) A, L, OE, R, E	(3) Real or Nominal	(4) Closed or Open	(5) Debit/ Credit

P4-7 Analyzing Financial Statements

1.

2.

3.

P4-8 Analyzing Financial Statements

1.

2.

3.

P4-11 Unifying Concepts: Adjusting and Closing Entries

1.–2.

JOURNAL

PAGE

	DATE	DESCRIPTION	POST REF.	DEBIT	CREDIT	
1						1
2						2
3						3
4						4
5						5
6						6
7						7
8						8
9						9
10						10
11						11
12						12
13						13
14						14
15						15
16						16
17						17
18						18
19						19
20						20
21						21
22						22
23						23
24						24
25						25
26						26
27						27
28						28
29						29
30						30
31						31
32						32

P4-12 Unifying Concepts: Analysis of Accounts

1.

2.

P4-12 Concluded

3.

4.

P4-13 Unifying Concepts: Analysis and Correction of Errors

P4-14 Unifying Concepts: The Accounting Cycle

1.

JOURNAL

PAGE

	DATE	DESCRIPTION	POST REF.	DEBIT	CREDIT	
1						1
2						2
3						3
4						4
5						5
6						6
7						7
8						8
9						9
10						10
11						11
12						12
13						13
14						14
15						15
16						16
17						17
18						18
19						19
20						20
21						21
22						22
23						23
24						24
25						25
26						26
27						27
28						28
29						29
30						30
31						31
32						32

P4-14 Continued

2.

Cash

Accounts Receivable

Land

Inventory

Notes Payable

Accounts Payable

Retained Earnings

Sales Revenue

Capital Stock

Interest Expense

Dividends

Salaries Expense

Cost of Goods Sold

P4-14 Continued

3.

P4-14 Continued

3. Continued

4.

JOURNAL

PAGE

	DATE		DESCRIPTION	POST REF.	DEBIT	CREDIT	
1							1
2							2
3							3
4							4
5							5
6							6
7							7
8							8
9							9
10							10
11							11
12							12
13							13
14							14
15							15
16							16
17							17
18							18

P4-14 Concluded

5.

Comprehensive Problem 1–5

1. Journalize current year transactions

JOURNAL PAGE

	DATE		DESCRIPTION	POST REF.	DEBIT	CREDIT	
1							1
2							2
3							3
4							4
5							5
6							6
7							7
8							8
9							9
10							10
11							11
12							12
13							13
14							14
15							15
16							16
17							17
18							18
19							19
20							20
21							21
22							22
23							23
24							24
25							25
26							26
27							27
28							28
29							29
30							30
31							31
32							32

Comp. Prob. 1–5 Continued

2. Post to T-accounts

Cash

Accounts Receivable

Inventory

Supplies

Prepaid Insurance

Prepaid Truck Rental

Accounts Payable

Salaries Payable

Interest Payable

Unearned Rent Revenue

Income Taxes Payable

Long-Term Bank Loan

Capital Stock

Retained Earnings

Sales Revenue

Comp. Prob. 1–5 Continued

2. Continued

Rent Revenue	

Cost of Goods Sold	

Supplies Expense	

Interest Expense	

Salaries Expense	

Miscellaneous Expense	

Income Tax Expense	

Comp. Prob. 1–5 Continued

3. Journalize and post adjusting entries

JOURNAL

PAGE

	DATE		DESCRIPTION	POST REF.	DEBIT	CREDIT	
1							1
2							2
3							3
4							4
5							5
6							6
7							7
8							8
9							9
10							10
11							11
12							12
13							13
14							14
15							15
16							16
17							17
18							18
19							19
20							20
21							21
22							22
23							23
24							24
25							25
26							26
27							27
28							28
29							29
30							30
31							31
32							32

Name ____________________

Comp. Prob. 1–5 Continued

4. Trial balance, balance sheet, and income statement

Comp. Prob. 1–5 Continued

4. Continued

Comp. Prob. 1–5 Continued

4. Continued

5. Journalize closing entries and prepare a post-closing trial balance

JOURNAL PAGE

	DATE		DESCRIPTION	POST REF.	DEBIT	CREDIT	
1							1
2							2
3							3
4							4
5							5
6							6
7							7
8							8
9							9
10							10

Comp. Prob. 1–5 Continued

5. Continued

6. Analysis using DuPont framework

Comp. Prob. 1–5 Concluded

7. Interpretive questions

P6-1 Recognizing Revenue

1.–2.

P6-2 Recognizing Revenue

1.–2.

P6-3 Sales Transactions

Company R—Seller

JOURNAL

PAGE

	DATE		DESCRIPTION	POST REF.	DEBIT	CREDIT	
1							1
2							2
3							3
4							4
5							5
6							6
7							7
8							8
9							9
10							10
11							11
12							12
13							13
14							14
15							15
16							16
17							17
18							18
19							19
20							20
21							21
22							22
23							23
24							24
25							25
26							26
27							27
28							28
29							29
30							30
31							31
32							32

P6-4 Cash Fraud

1.–2.

P6-5 Analysis of Allowance for Bad Debts

1.

JOURNAL PAGE

	DATE		DESCRIPTION	POST REF.	DEBIT	CREDIT	
1							1
2							2
3							3
4							4
5							5
6							6
7							7
8							8
9							9
10							10
11							11
12							12
13							13
14							14

P6-5 Concluded

2.

JOURNAL PAGE

	DATE		DESCRIPTION	POST REF.	DEBIT	CREDIT	
1							1
2							2
3							3
4							4
5							5
6							6
7							7
8							8
9							9
10							10
11							11
12							12
13							13
14							14
15							15
16							16
17							17
18							18
19							19
20							20
21							21
22							22
23							23
24							24
25							25
26							26
27							27
28							28
29							29
30							30
31							31
32							32

Name ______________________________

P6-6 Accounting for Accounts Receivable

1.

JOURNAL

PAGE

	DATE	DESCRIPTION	POST REF.	DEBIT	CREDIT	
1						1
2						2
3						3
4						4
5						5
6						6
7						7
8						8
9						9
10						10
11						11
12						12
13						13
14						14
15						15
16						16
17						17
18						18
19						19
20						20
21						21
22						22
23						23
24						24
25						25
26						26
27						27
28						28
29						29
30						30
31						31
32						32

P6-6 Concluded

2.

P6-7 Analysis of Receivables

1.–2.

P6-9 Unifying Concepts: Aging of Accounts Receivable and Uncollectible Accounts

1.

JOURNAL PAGE

	DATE		DESCRIPTION	POST REF.	DEBIT	CREDIT	
1							1
2							2
3							3
4							4
5							5

2.–3.

JOURNAL PAGE

	DATE		DESCRIPTION	POST REF.	DEBIT	CREDIT	
1							1
2							2
3							3
4							4
5							5
6							6
7							7
8							8
9							9
10							10
11							11
12							12

P6-9 Concluded

4.

JOURNAL PAGE

	DATE		DESCRIPTION	POST REF.	DEBIT	CREDIT	
1							1
2							2
3							3
4							4
5							5
6							6
7							7
8							8
9							9
10							10
11							11
12							12
13							13
14							14
15							15
16							16
17							17

Name ________________________________

P6-10 Estimating Uncollectible Accounts

1.

JOURNAL

PAGE

	DATE	DESCRIPTION	POST REF.	DEBIT	CREDIT	
1						1
2						2
3						3
4						4
5						5

2.

JOURNAL

PAGE

	DATE	DESCRIPTION	POST REF.	DEBIT	CREDIT	
1						1
2						2
3						3
4						4
5						5

P6-10 Continued

3.

JOURNAL PAGE

	DATE		DESCRIPTION	POST REF.	DEBIT	CREDIT	
1							1
2							2
3							3
4							4
5							5
6							6
7							7
8							8
9							9
10							10

4.

JOURNAL PAGE

	DATE		DESCRIPTION	POST REF.	DEBIT	CREDIT	
1							1
2							2
3							3
4							4
5							5
6							6
7							7
8							8
9							9
10							10
11							11
12							12
13							13
14							14
15							15
16							16
17							17
18							18

P6-10 Concluded

5.

P6-11 The Aging Method

1.

Category	Amount	Percentage	Total

2.

JOURNAL PAGE

	DATE		DESCRIPTION	POST REF.	DEBIT	CREDIT	
1							1
2							2
3							3
4							4
5							5

3.

Name ________________________________

P6-14 Determining Where the Cash Went

1.–2.

P6-15 Accounting for a Note Receivable

1.

JOURNAL PAGE

	DATE		DESCRIPTION	POST REF.	DEBIT	CREDIT	
1							1
2							2
3							3
4							4
5							5
6							6
7							7
8							8
9							9
10							10
11							11
12							12
13							13
14							14

2.

Name ______________________________

P6-16 Accounting for a Note Receivable

1.–3.

JOURNAL PAGE

	DATE		DESCRIPTION	POST REF.	DEBIT	CREDIT	
1							1
2							2
3							3
4							4
5							5
6							6
7							7
8							8
9							9
10							10
11							11
12							12
13							13
14							14
15							15
16							16
17							17
18							18
19							19
20							20
21							21
22							22
23							23
24							24
25							25
26							26
27							27
28							28
29							29
30							30
31							31
32							32

P6-17 Accounting for a Foreign Currency Transaction

1.–3.

JOURNAL PAGE

DATE		DESCRIPTION	POST REF.	DEBIT	CREDIT

P6-17 Concluded

4.

P7-3 Income Statement Calculations

P7-4 Income Statement Calculations

	Company A	Company B	Company C	Company D

P7-5 Inventory Cost Flow Alternatives

1.

a. FIFO

	UNITS	TOTAL COST

P7-5 Continued

b. LIFO

		UNITS	TOTAL COST

P7-5 Concluded

c. Average cost

	UNITS	TOTAL COST

2.

P7-6 Periodic Inventory Cost Flow Method

1.

2.

3.

P7-7 Calculating and Interpreting Inventory Ratios

1.

2.

P7-8 The Effect of Inventory Errors

1.

2.

3.

P7-9 Correction of Inventory Errors

P7-10 The Effect of Inventory Errors

1.

2.

P7-11 Unifying Concepts: Inventory Cost Flow Alternatives

1.

2.

Name ____________________

P8-3 Stock Options

1.–4.

P8-4 Accounting for Pensions

1.–3.

Name ______________________________

P8-5 Accounting for Pensions

1.

Year	Interest Cost	Service Cost	Pension Fund Return	Pension Expense

2.

Year	Year-End Obligation	Year-End Plan Assets	Net Asset (Liability)

3.

4.

P8-6 Life Cycle of a Deferred Tax Item

1.–4.

P8-8 Income Statement Analysis

	2003	2002	2001
Gross sales revenue	$42,000	(9)	$25,800
Sales discounts	-0-	100	100
Sales returns	-0-	200	700
Net sales revenue	42,000	(10)	(1)
Beginning inventory	(15)	8,000	(2)
Purchases	24,800	(11)	15,000
Purchase discounts	700	300	500
Freight-in	(16)	-0-	500
Cost of goods available for sale	29,000	25,000	(3)
Ending inventory	3,800	(12)	(4)
Cost of goods sold	(17)	(13)	(5)
Gross margin (40%)	(18)	14,000	(6)
Selling expenses	4,000	(14)	(7)
General and administrative expenses	(19)	3,200	3,000
Income before income taxes	9,000	8,000	4,000
Income taxes	4,500	4,000	(8)
Net income	(20)	4,000	2,000

Comprehensive Problem 6–8

1. Journal entries

JOURNAL PAGE

	DATE		DESCRIPTION	POST REF.	DEBIT	CREDIT	
1							1
2							2
3							3
4							4
5							5
6							6
7							7
8							8
9							9
10							10
11							11
12							12
13							13
14							14
15							15
16							16
17							17
18							18
19							19
20							20
21							21
22							22
23							23
24							24
25							25
26							26
27							27
28							28
29							29
30							30
31							31
32							32

Comp. Prob. 6–8 Continued

1. Continued

JOURNAL

PAGE

	DATE		DESCRIPTION	POST REF.	DEBIT	CREDIT	
1							1
2							2
3							3
4							4
5							5
6							6
7							7
8							8
9							9
10							10
11							11
12							12
13							13
14							14
15							15
16							16
17							17
18							18
19							19
20							20
21							21
22							22
23							23
24							24
25							25
26							26
27							27
28							28
29							29
30							30
31							31
32							32

Comp. Prob. 6–8 Continued

1. Concluded

JOURNAL

PAGE

	DATE		DESCRIPTION	POST REF.	DEBIT	CREDIT	
1							1
2							2
3							3
4							4
5							5
6							6
7							7
8							8
9							9
10							10
11							11
12							12
13							13
14							14

2. Adjusting entries

JOURNAL

PAGE

	DATE		DESCRIPTION	POST REF.	DEBIT	CREDIT	
1							1
2							2
3							3
4							4
5							5
6							6
7							7
8							8
9							9
10							10
11							11
12							12
13							13
14							14

Comp. Prob. 6–8 Continued

2. Concluded

3. Trial balance

Comp. Prob. 6–8 Continued

4. Income statement and balance sheet

Comp. Prob. 6–8 Concluded

5. Common-size income statement

6.

P9-4 Accounting for Leased Assets

1. ____________________

2.

JOURNAL PAGE

	DATE		DESCRIPTION	POST REF.	DEBIT	CREDIT	
1							1
2							2
3							3
4							4
5							5
6							6
7							7
8							8
9							9
10							10

3.

JOURNAL PAGE

	DATE		DESCRIPTION	POST REF.	DEBIT	CREDIT	
1							1
2							2
3							3
4							4
5							5
6							6
7							7
8							8

P9-5 Accounting for Leased Assets

1.

2.

JOURNAL PAGE

	DATE	DESCRIPTION	POST REF.	DEBIT	CREDIT	
1						1
2						2
3						3
4						4
5						5
6						6
7						7
8						8
9						9
10						10
11						11
12						12
13						13
14						14
15						15

P9-6 Interest Capitalization

1.

2.

P9-7 Depreciation Calculations

1.

2.

3.

JOURNAL PAGE

	DATE		DESCRIPTION	POST REF.	DEBIT	CREDIT	
1							1
2							2
3							3
4							4
5							5

P9-8 Purchase of Multiple Assets for a Single Sum

1.–4.

JOURNAL

PAGE

	DATE		DESCRIPTION	POST REF.	DEBIT	CREDIT	
1							1
2							2
3							3
4							4
5							5
6							6
7							7
8							8
9							9
10							10
11							11
12							12
13							13
14							14
15							15
16							16
17							17
18							18
19							19
20							20
21							21
22							22
23							23
24							24

Name ______________________________

P9-9 Basket Purchase and Partial-Year Depreciation

1.

JOURNAL PAGE

	DATE		DESCRIPTION	POST REF.	DEBIT	CREDIT	
1							1
2							2
3							3
4							4
5							5
6							6
7							7
8							8
9							9
10							10

2.

P9-10 Acquisition, Depreciation, and Sale of an Asset

1.

JOURNAL PAGE

	DATE		DESCRIPTION	POST REF.	DEBIT	CREDIT	
1							1
2							2
3							3
4							4
5							5
6							6
7							7
8							8

2.

3.

JOURNAL PAGE

	DATE		DESCRIPTION	POST REF.	DEBIT	CREDIT	
1							1
2							2
3							3
4							4
5							5
6							6
7							7
8							8
9							9
10							10
11							11
12							12
13							13
14							14

P9-11 Acquisition, Depreciation, and Sale of an Asset

1.

JOURNAL PAGE

	DATE		DESCRIPTION	POST REF.	DEBIT	CREDIT	
1							1
2							2
3							3
4							4
5							5
6							6
7							7
8							8
9							9
10							10
11							11
12							12
13							13
14							14
15							15
16							16
17							17
18							18
19							19
20							20
21							21

2.–3.

P9-12 Accounting for Natural Resources

1.–3.

JOURNAL PAGE

	DATE	DESCRIPTION	POST REF.	DEBIT	CREDIT	
1						1
2						2
3						3
4						4
5						5
6						6
7						7
8						8
9						9
10						10
11						11
12						12
13						13
14						14

P9-13 Asset Impairment

1.–2.

Name ________________________________

P9-14 Accounting for Intangible Assets (Goodwill)

1.–2.

JOURNAL

PAGE

DATE	DESCRIPTION	POST REF.	DEBIT	CREDIT

P9-15 Accounting for Goodwill

1.–4.

Name ____________________

P9-19 Financial Statement Effects of Depreciation Models

1.–3.

P9-20 Depreciation Calculations

1.–3.

P9-20 Concluded

4.–5.

P9-21 Changes in Depreciation Estimates and Capitalization of Expenditures

1a.–c.

JOURNAL

PAGE

DATE		DESCRIPTION	POST REF.	DEBIT	CREDIT

P9-21 Concluded

1.d–e.

JOURNAL PAGE

	DATE		DESCRIPTION	POST REF.	DEBIT	CREDIT	
1							1
2							2
3							3
4							4
5							5
6							6
7							7
8							8
9							9
10							10
11							11
12							12
13							13
14							14
15							15
16							16
17							17
18							18

2.

P9-22 Unifying Concepts: Accounting for Natural Resources

1.

JOURNAL PAGE

	DATE		DESCRIPTION	POST REF.	DEBIT	CREDIT	
1							1
2							2
3							3
4							4
5							5
6							6
7							7
8							8
9							9
10							10
11							11
12							12
13							13
14							14
15							15
16							16
17							17
18							18
19							19
20							20
21							21
22							22
23							23
24							24
25							25
26							26
27							27
28							28
29							29
30							30
31							31
32							32

P9-22 Concluded

2.

3.

P9-23 Unifying Concepts: Property, Plant, and Equipment

1.–4.

JOURNAL

PAGE

	DATE		DESCRIPTION	POST REF.	DEBIT	CREDIT	
1							1
2							2
3							3
4							4
5							5
6							6
7							7
8							8
9							9
10							10
11							11
12							12
13							13
14							14
15							15
16							16
17							17
18							18
19							19
20							20
21							21
22							22
23							23
24							24
25							25
26							26
27							27
28							28
29							29
30							30
31							31
32							32

P10-1 Present and Future Value Computations

1.–2.

P10-2 Present and Future Value Computations

1.–2.

P10-3 Computing the Amount of Periodic Payments

1.–3.

P10-4 Accounting for Notes Payable

JOURNAL

PAGE

	DATE		DESCRIPTION	POST REF.	DEBIT	CREDIT	
1							1
2							2
3							3
4							4
5							5
6							6
7							7
8							8
9							9
10							10
11							11
12							12
13							13
14							14
15							15
16							16
17							17
18							18
19							19
20							20
21							21
22							22
23							23
24							24
25							25
26							26
27							27
28							28
29							29
30							30
31							31
32							32

P10-4 Concluded

JOURNAL

PAGE

DATE	DESCRIPTION	POST REF.	DEBIT	CREDIT

P10-5 Accounting for Notes Payable

1.–3.

JOURNAL

PAGE

	DATE	DESCRIPTION	POST REF.	DEBIT	CREDIT	
1						1
2						2
3						3
4						4
5						5
6						6
7						7
8						8
9						9
10						10
11						11
12						12
13						13
14						14
15						15
16						16
17						17
18						18
19						19
20						20
21						21
22						22
23						23
24						24
25						25
26						26
27						27
28						28
29						29
30						30
31						31
32						32

P10-12 Reporting Liabilities on the Balance Sheet

P10-13 Reporting Liabilities on the Balance Sheet

P10-14 Computation of Debt-Related Financial Ratios

1.–5.

P10-15 Impact of Capitalizing the Value of Operating Leases

1.–5.

Name ______________________________

P10-16 Accounting for Bonds

1.–2.

JOURNAL

PAGE

	DATE		DESCRIPTION	POST REF.	DEBIT	CREDIT	
1							1
2							2
3							3
4							4
5							5
6							6
7							7
8							8
9							9
10							10
11							11
12							12
13							13
14							14
15							15
16							16
17							17
18							18
19							19
20							20
21							21
22							22
23							23
24							24
25							25
26							26
27							27
28							28
29							29
30							30
31							31
32							32

P10-16 Concluded

3.

4.

P10-17 Accounting for Bonds Issued at a Premium

1.–4.

JOURNAL

PAGE

DATE		DESCRIPTION	POST REF.	DEBIT	CREDIT

P10-18 Bonds Retired at Maturity

1.–4.

JOURNAL PAGE

DATE		DESCRIPTION	POST REF.	DEBIT	CREDIT

P10-19 Straight-Line versus Effective-Interest Amortization

1.–2.

P10-19 Continued

3.

P10-19 Concluded

4.–5.

JOURNAL

PAGE

	DATE	DESCRIPTION	POST REF.	DEBIT	CREDIT	
1						1
2						2
3						3
4						4
5						5
6						6
7						7
8						8
9						9
10						10
11						11
12						12
13						13
14						14

6.

P10-20 Effective-Interest Amortization

1.–2.

P10-20 Concluded

3.

JOURNAL

PAGE

	DATE		DESCRIPTION	POST REF.	DEBIT	CREDIT	
1							1
2							2
3							3
4							4
5							5
6							6
7							7
8							8
9							9
10							10
11							11
12							12
13							13
14							14
15							15

4.

P10-21 Accounting for Bonds

1.

JOURNAL PAGE

	DATE		DESCRIPTION	POST REF.	DEBIT	CREDIT	
1							1
2							2
3							3
4							4
5							5
6							6
7							7
8							8
9							9

2.

3.

Name ______________________________

P10-22 Straight-Line versus Effective-Interest Amortization

1.–3.

P10-22 Concluded

4.–6.

JOURNAL

PAGE

	DATE		DESCRIPTION	POST REF.	DEBIT	CREDIT	
1							1
2							2
3							3
4							4
5							5
6							6
7							7
8							8
9							9
10							10
11							11
12							12
13							13
14							14
15							15
16							16
17							17
18							18
19							19
20							20
21							21
22							22
23							23
24							24
25							25
26							26
27							27
28							28
29							29
30							30
31							31
32							32

Name ____________________

P10-23 Bonds Retired before Maturity

1.–2.

JOURNAL

PAGE

	DATE	DESCRIPTION	POST REF.	DEBIT	CREDIT	
1						1
2						2
3						3
4						4
5						5
6						6
7						7
8						8
9						9
10						10
11						11
12						12
13						13
14						14
15						15
16						16
17						17
18						18
19						19
20						20
21						21
22						22
23						23
24						24
25						25
26						26
27						27
28						28
29						29
30						30
31						31
32						32

P10-24 Unifying Concepts: Accounting for Bonds Payable

1.–2.

P10-24 Continued

3.

JOURNAL

PAGE

	DATE	DESCRIPTION	POST REF.	DEBIT	CREDIT	
1						1
2						2
3						3
4						4
5						5
6						6
7						7
8						8
9						9
10						10
11						11
12						12
13						13
14						14
15						15
16						16
17						17
18						18
19						19
20						20
21						21
22						22
23						23
24						24
25						25
26						26
27						27
28						28
29						29
30						30
31						31
32						32

P10-24 Concluded

4.–6.

P10-25 Analysis of Bonds

	Case 1	Case 2	Case 3
Case received at issuance date			
Total cash paid to bondholders through maturity			
Income Statement for 2003:			
Bond interest expense			
Balance Sheet at Dec. 31 2003:			
Long-term liabilities:			
Bonds payable, 12%			
Unamortized discount			
Unamortized premium			
Bond carrying value			
Approximate effective interest rate			

Calculations:

Name ____________________

P11-1 Stock Transactions and Analysis

JOURNAL

	DATE		DESCRIPTION	POST REF.	DEBIT	CREDIT	
1	1.	(a)					1
2							2
3							3
4							4
5							5
6							6
7							7

(b) ____________________

	DATE		DESCRIPTION	POST REF.	DEBIT	CREDIT	
1	2.	(a)					1
2							2
3							3
4							4
5							5
6							6
7							7

(b) ____________________

	DATE		DESCRIPTION	POST REF.	DEBIT	CREDIT	
1	3.	(a)					1
2							2
3							3
4							4
5							5
6							6
7							7

(b) ____________________

P11-1 Concluded

JOURNAL

DATE		DESCRIPTION	POST REF.	DEBIT	CREDIT
4.	(a)				

(b) ____________________

DATE		DESCRIPTION	POST REF.	DEBIT	CREDIT
5.	(a)				

(b) ____________________

Name ____

P11-2 Stock Transactions and the Stockholders' Equity Section

1.

JOURNAL

PAGE

	DATE		DESCRIPTION	POST REF.	DEBIT	CREDIT	
1							1
2							2
3							3
4							4
5							5
6							6
7							7
8							8
9							9
10							10
11							11
12							12
13							13
14							14
15							15
16							16
17							17
18							18
19							19
20							20
21							21
22							22
23							23
24							24
25							25
26							26
27							27
28							28
29							29
30							30
31							31
32							32

P11-2 Continued

2.

P11-2 Concluded

2. *Calculations*

Preferred Stock

Common Stock

Paid-In Capital in Excess of Par, Preferred Stock

Paid-In Capital in Excess of Par, Common Stock

Treasury Stock

Paid-in Capital, Treasury Stock

Retained Earnings

P11-3 Recording Stockholders' Equity Transactions

JOURNAL

PAGE

DATE		DESCRIPTION	POST REF.	DEBIT	CREDIT

P11-5 Stockholders' Equity, Dividends, and Treasury Stock

1.

JOURNAL

PAGE

DATE	DESCRIPTION	POST REF.	DEBIT	CREDIT

P11-5 Continued

1. Continued

JOURNAL

PAGE

	DATE		DESCRIPTION	POST REF.	DEBIT	CREDIT	
1							1
2							2
3							3
4							4
5							5
6							6
7							7
8							8
9							9
10							10
11							11
12							12
13							13
14							14
15							15
16							16
17							17
18							18
19							19
20							20
21							21
22							22
23							23
24							24
25							25
26							26
27							27
28							28
29							29
30							30
31							31
32							32

P11-5 Continued

2.

P11-5 Concluded

2. *Calculations*

Preferred Stock

Common Stock

Paid-In Capital in Excess of Par, Preferred Stock

Paid-In Capital in Excess of Par, Common Stock

Retained Earnings

Treasury Stock

Paid-In Capital, Treasury Stock

Dividends, Common Stock

Dividends, Preferred Stock

3.

P11-8 Dividend Payout Ratio

1. A B C

2.

P11-9 Preparing the Stockholder's Equity Section and Recording Dividends

1.

P11-9 Concluded

2.

JOURNAL

PAGE

	DATE		DESCRIPTION	POST REF.	DEBIT	CREDIT	
1							1
2							2
3							3
4							4
5							5
6							6
7							7
8							8
9							9
10							10

P11-10 Stockholders' Equity Calculations

1.

JOURNAL PAGE

	DATE		DESCRIPTION	POST REF.	DEBIT	CREDIT	
1							1
2							2
3							3
4							4
5							5
6							6
7							7
8							8
9							9
10							10
11							11
12							12
13							13
14							14
15							15

2.

P11-11 Stock Calculations and the Stockholders' Equity Section

1.–2.

3.

P11-12 Unifying Concepts: Stock Transactions and the Stockholders' Equity Section

1.

JOURNAL PAGE

	DATE		DESCRIPTION	POST REF.	DEBIT	CREDIT	
1							1
2							2
3							3
4							4
5							5
6							6
7							7
8							8
9							9
10							10
11							11
12							12
13							13
14							14
15							15
16							16
17							17
18							18
19							19
20							20
21							21
22							22
23							23
24							24
25							25
26							26
27							27
28							28

Name ______________________________

P11-12 Continued

1. Concluded

JOURNAL

PAGE

	DATE	DESCRIPTION	POST REF.	DEBIT	CREDIT	
1						1
2						2
3						3
4						4
5						5
6						6
7						7
8						8
9						9
10						10
11						11
12						12
13						13
14						14
15						15
16						16
17						17
18						18
19						19
20						20
21						21
22						22
23						23
24						24
25						25
26						26
27						27
28						28
29						29
30						30
31						31
32						32

P11-12 Continued

2.

P11-12 Concluded

2. *Calculations:*

Common Stock

Preferred Stock

Paid-In Capital in Excess of Par, Common Stock

Common Stock, No Par

Paid-In Capital in Excess of Par, Preferred Stock

Treasury Stock, Common, No Par

Treasury Stock, Common

Paid-In Capital, Treasury Stock

Retained Earnings

P11-13 Unifying Concepts: Stock Transactions, the Stockholders' Equity Section, and the Statement of Stockholders' Equity

1.

JOURNAL

PAGE

	DATE		DESCRIPTION	POST REF.	DEBIT	CREDIT	
1							1
2							2
3							3
4							4
5							5
6							6
7							7
8							8
9							9
10							10
11							11
12							12
13							13
14							14
15							15
16							16
17							17
18							18
19							19
20							20
21							21
22							22
23							23
24							24
25							25
26							26
27							27
28							28
29							29
30							30
31							31
32							32

P11-13 Continued

2.

P11-13 Continued

2. *Calculations:*

Common Stock

Paid-In Capital in Excess of Par, Common Stock

Treasury Stock

Paid-In Capital, Treasury Stock

Retained Earnings

P11-13 Concluded

3.

	Common Stock Issued		Paid-In Capital in Excess of Par, Common Stock	Retained Earnings	Treasury Stock	Paid-In Capital, Treasury Stock	Total Stockholder's Equity
	Shares	$ Amount					

P11-14 Unifying Concepts: Stockholders' Equity

1.

JOURNAL

PAGE

	DATE	DESCRIPTION	POST REF.	DEBIT	CREDIT	
1						1
2						2
3						3
4						4
5						5
6						6
7						7
8						8
9						9
10						10
11						11
12						12
13						13
14						14
15						15
16						16
17						17
18						18
19						19
20						20
21						21
22						22
23						23
24						24
25						25
26						26
27						27
28						28
29						29
30						30
31						31
32						32

P11-14 Continued

P11-14 Concluded

2. ***Calculations:***

Preferred Stock	

Common Stock	

Paid-In Capital in Excess of Par, Preferred Stock	

Paid-In Capital in Excess of Par, Common Stock	

Treasury Stock	

Paid-In Capital, Treasury Stock	

Retained Earnings	

P11-15 Comprehensive Income

1.

2.

P11-16 Stockholders' Equity Section with Selected "Other Information"

1.–4.

P11-17 Recording Stockholders' Equity Transactions

JOURNAL

PAGE

	DATE		DESCRIPTION	POST REF.	DEBIT	CREDIT	
1							1
2							2
3							3
4							4
5							5
6							6
7							7
8							8
9							9
10							10
11							11
12							12
13							13
14							14
15							15
16							16
17							17
18							18
19							19
20							20
21							21
22							22
23							23
24							24
25							25
26							26
27							27
28							28
29							29
30							30
31							31
32							32

P11-18 Dividend Transactions and Calculations

1.

JOURNAL PAGE

	DATE	DESCRIPTION	POST REF.	DEBIT	CREDIT	
1						1
2						2
3						3
4						4
5						5
6						6
7						7
8						8
9						9
10						10
11						11
12						12
13						13
14						14
15						15
16						16
17						17
18						18
19						19
20						20
21						21
22						22
23						23
24						24
25						25
26						26
27						27
28						28
29						29
30						30
31						31
32						32

P11-18 Concluded

2.–3.

P11-19 Recording Dividend Transactions and Reporting Stockholders' Equity

1.

JOURNAL PAGE

DATE	DESCRIPTION	POST REF.	DEBIT	CREDIT

P11-19 Continued

2.

Use the form on the next page to prepare the statement of stockholders' equity

3.

P11-19 Concluded

3. Concluded

	Preferred Stock		Common Stock		Paid-In Capital in Excess of Par, Common Stock	Retained Earnings	Total Stockholder's Equity
	Shares	$ Amount	Shares	$ Amount			

Name ____________________

P11-20 Statement of Retained Earnings and Stockhoders' Equity

1.

2.

P11-21 Statement of Retained Earnings

P11-22 Accounting for a Proprietorship

1.

JOURNAL

PAGE

	DATE		DESCRIPTION	POST REF.	DEBIT	CREDIT	
1							1
2							2
3							3
4							4
5							5
6							6
7							7
8							8
9							9
10							10
11							11
12							12
13							13
14							14

P11-22 Concluded

2.

3.

P11-23 Partnership Accounting

1.

JOURNAL PAGE

	DATE	DESCRIPTION	POST REF.	DEBIT	CREDIT	
1						1
2						2
3						3
4						4
5						5
6						6
7						7
8						8
9						9
10						10
11						11
12						12
13						13
14						14
15						15
16						16
17						17
18						18
19						19
20						20
21						21
22						22
23						23
24						24
25						25
26						26
27						27
28						28
29						29
30						30
31						31
32						32

P11-23 Continued

2.

JOURNAL

PAGE

DATE		DESCRIPTION	POST REF.	DEBIT	CREDIT

P11-23 Concluded

3.–4.

P12-1 Investment in Securities—Recording and Analysis

JOURNAL

PAGE

DATE	DESCRIPTION	POST REF.	DEBIT	CREDIT

P12-1 Concluded

JOURNAL

PAGE

	DATE		DESCRIPTION	POST REF.	DEBIT	CREDIT	
1							1
2							2
3							3
4							4
5							5
6							6

Cash

Investment in Trading Securities—Corporation A Stock

Investment in Trading Securities—Corporation B Bonds

Bond Interest Receivable

Investment in Available-for-Sale Securities—Corporation C Stock

Bond Interest Revenue

Dividend Revenue

Realized Loss on Sale of Trading Securities

Realized Gain on Sale of Trading Securities

P12-2 Buying and Selling Trading Securities

1.–2.

P12-3 Trading and Available-for-Sale Securities

1.–2.

P12-4 Investments in Trading Securities

JOURNAL

PAGE

	DATE	DESCRIPTION	POST REF.	DEBIT	CREDIT	
1						1
2						2
3						3
4						4
5						5
6						6
7						7
8						8
9						9
10						10
11						11
12						12
13						13
14						14
15						15
16						16
17						17
18						18
19						19
20						20
21						21
22						22
23						23
24						24
25						25
26						26
27						27
28						28
29						29
30						30
31						31
32						32

P12-5 Investments in Debt and Equity Securities

1.

JOURNAL PAGE

	DATE	DESCRIPTION	POST REF.	DEBIT	CREDIT	
1						1
2						2
3						3
4						4
5						5
6						6
7						7
8						8
9						9
10						10
11						11
12						12
13						13
14						14
15						15
16						16
17						17
18						18
19						19

P12-5 Concluded

2.

3.

P12-6 Unifying Concepts: Short-Term Investments in Stocks and Bonds

JOURNAL

PAGE

DATE		DESCRIPTION	POST REF.	DEBIT	CREDIT

P12-6 Concluded

JOURNAL

PAGE

	DATE		DESCRIPTION	POST REF.	DEBIT	CREDIT	
1							1
2							2
3							3
4							4
5							5
6							6
7							7
8							8
9							9
10							10
11							11
12							12
13							13
14							14
15							15
16							16
17							17
18							18
19							19

P12-7 Recording Investment Transactions

Cash	

Investment in Trading Securities, Corporation A Stock	

Dividend Revenue	

Investment in Trading Securities, Corporation B Bonds	

Bond Interest Revenue	

Investment in Available-for-Sale Securities	

Bond Interest Receivable	

Realized Loss on Sale of Trading Securities	

Name ______________________

P12-7 Concluded

Unrealized Gain on Trading Securities—Income	

Unrealized Increase/Decrease in Value of Available-for-Sale Securities—Equity	

Market Adjustment—Trading Securities	

Market Adjustment—Available-for-Sale Securities	

P12-8 Investments in Available-for-Sale Securities

1.

P12-8 Concluded

1. Concluded

JOURNAL PAGE

	DATE		DESCRIPTION	POST REF.	DEBIT	CREDIT	
1							1
2							2
3							3
4							4
5							5
6							6
7							7
8							8
9							9
10							10
11							11
12							12

2.

3. **JOURNAL** PAGE

	DATE		DESCRIPTION	POST REF.	DEBIT	CREDIT	
1							1
2							2
3							3
4							4

4.

Name ______________________________

P12-9 Unifying Concepts: Investments in Debt and Equity Securities

1.

JOURNAL

PAGE

	DATE		DESCRIPTION	POST REF.	DEBIT	CREDIT	
1							1
2							2
3							3
4							4
5							5
6							6
7							7
8							8
9							9
10							10
11							11
12							12
13							13
14							14
15							15
16							16
17							17
18							18
19							19
20							20
21							21
22							22
23							23
24							24
25							25
26							26
27							27
28							28
29							29
30							30
31							31
32							32

P12-9 Concluded

2.

P12-10 Investments in Equity Securities

1.

2.

JOURNAL PAGE

	DATE		DESCRIPTION	POST REF.	DEBIT	CREDIT	
1							1
2							2
3							3
4							4
5							5
6							6
7							7
8							8
9							9
10							10
11							11
12							12
13							13
14							14
15							15

P12-10 Concluded

3.

P12-11 Investment Portfolio

1.

JOURNAL

PAGE

	DATE		DESCRIPTION	POST REF.	DEBIT	CREDIT	
1							1
2							2
3							3
4							4
5							5
6							6
7							7
8							8
9							9
10							10
11							11
12							12
13							13
14							14

2.

P12-11 Concluded

3.

JOURNAL PAGE

	DATE		DESCRIPTION	POST REF.	DEBIT	CREDIT	
1							1
2							2
3							3
4							4
5							5
6							6
7							7
8							8

4.

JOURNAL PAGE

	DATE		DESCRIPTION	POST REF.	DEBIT	CREDIT	
1							1
2							2
3							3
4							4
5							5
6							6
7							7
8							8
9							9
10							10

P12-12 Investments in Held-to-Maturity Securities

1.

JOURNAL

PAGE

	DATE		DESCRIPTION	POST REF.	DEBIT	CREDIT	
1							1
2							2
3							3
4							4
5							5
6							6
7							7
8							8
9							9
10							10
11							11
12							12
13							13
14							14
15							15
16							16
17							17
18							18
19							19
20							20
21							21
22							22
23							23
24							24
25							25
26							26
27							27
28							28
29							29
30							30
31							31
32							32

P12-12 Continued

1. Continued

JOURNAL

PAGE

	DATE		DESCRIPTION	POST REF.	DEBIT	CREDIT	
1							1
2							2
3							3
4							4
5							5
6							6
7							7
8							8
9							9
10							10
11							11
12							12
13							13
14							14
15							15
16							16
17							17
18							18
19							19
20							20
21							21
22							22
23							23
24							24
25							25
26							26
27							27
28							28
29							29
30							30
31							31
32							32

P12-12 Concluded

1. Concluded

JOURNAL

PAGE

	DATE		DESCRIPTION	POST REF.	DEBIT	CREDIT	
1							1
2							2
3							3
4							4
5							5
6							6
7							7
8							8
9							9
10							10
11							11
12							12
13							13
14							14
15							15

2.

P12-13 Investments in Held-to-Maturity Securities

1. ______

2. ______

3. ______

4. ______

5. ______

P12-14 Determining the Purchase Price of Held-to-Maturity Securities and Effective-Interest Amortization

1.–2.

P12-14 Concluded

3.–4.

P12-15 Investments in Held-to-Maturity Securities

1.

JOURNAL PAGE

	DATE	DESCRIPTION	POST REF.	DEBIT	CREDIT	
1						1
2						2
3						3
4						4
5						5
6						6
7						7
8						8
9						9
10						10
11						11
12						12
13						13
14						14
15						15
16						16
17						17
18						18
19						19
20						20
21						21
22						22
23						23
24						24
25						25
26						26
27						27
28						28
29						29
30						30
31						31
32						32

Name ____________________

P12-15 Concluded

2.

JOURNAL

PAGE

	DATE		DESCRIPTION	POST REF.	DEBIT	CREDIT	
1							1
2							2
3							3
4							4
5							5
6							6
7							7
8							8
9							9
10							10
11							11
12							12
13							13
14							14
15							15
16							16
17							17
18							18
19							19
20							20
21							21
22							22
23							23
24							24
25							25
26							26
27							27
28							28
29							29
30							30
31							31
32							32

P12-16 Long-Term Investments in Equity Securities

1.

2.

JOURNAL

PAGE

	DATE		DESCRIPTION	POST REF.	DEBIT	CREDIT	
1							1
2							2
3							3
4							4
5							5
6							6
7							7
8							8
9							9
10							10
11							11
12							12
13							13
14							14
15							15
16							16
17							17
18							18
19							19
20							20
21							21
22							22
23							23
24							24
25							25
26							26
27							27

Name ______________________________

P12-17 Investments in Stocks—Equity Method

1.

2.

JOURNAL PAGE

	DATE		DESCRIPTION	POST REF.	DEBIT	CREDIT	
1							1
2							2
3							3
4							4
5							5
6							6
7							7
8							8
9							9
10							10
11							11
12							12
13							13
14							14
15							15

P12-18 Long-Term Investments in Stock—Available-for-Sale and Equity Method

1.

JOURNAL

PAGE

DATE	DESCRIPTION	POST REF.	DEBIT	CREDIT

P12-18 Continued

1. Concluded

JOURNAL

PAGE

DATE		DESCRIPTION	POST REF.	DEBIT	CREDIT

P12-18 Concluded

2.

3.

P12-19 Long-Term Investments in Equity Securities

1.

P12-19 Concluded

2.

JOURNAL

PAGE

	DATE		DESCRIPTION	POST REF.	DEBIT	CREDIT	
1							1
2							2
3							3
4							4
5							5
6							6
7							7
8							8
9							9
10							10
11							11
12							12
13							13
14							14
15							15
16							16
17							17
18							18
19							19
20							20
21							21
22							22
23							23
24							24
25							25
26							26
27							27
28							28
29							29
30							30
31							31
32							32

P12-20 Unifying Concepts: Long-Term Investments in Stocks and Bonds

1.

JOURNAL

PAGE

DATE		DESCRIPTION	POST REF.	DEBIT	CREDIT

P12-20 Continued

1. Concluded

JOURNAL

PAGE

	DATE		DESCRIPTION	POST REF.	DEBIT	CREDIT	
1							1
2							2
3							3
4							4
5							5
6							6
7							7
8							8
9							9
10							10
11							11
12							12
13							13
14							14
15							15
16							16
17							17
18							18
19							19
20							20
21							21
22							22
23							23
24							24
25							25
26							26
27							27
28							28
29							29
30							30
31							31
32							32

P12-20 Concluded

2.

Comprehensive Problem 3

1. Journal entries for 2002

JOURNAL PAGE

	DATE		DESCRIPTION	POST REF.	DEBIT	CREDIT	
1							1
2							2
3							3
4							4
5							5
6							6
7							7
8							8
9							9
10							10
11							11
12							12
13							13
14							14
15							15
16							16
17							17
18							18
19							19
20							20
21							21
22							22
23							23
24							24
25							25
26							26
27							27
28							28
29							29
30							30
31							31
32							32

Comp. Prob. 3 Continued

Concluded

JOURNAL

PAGE

DATE		DESCRIPTION	POST REF.	DEBIT	CREDIT

Comp. Prob. 3 Continued

2. Trial balance

Comp. Prob. 3 Continued

3. Financial statements for 2002

Name ______________________

Comp. Prob. 3 Continued

3. Concluded

Comp. Prob. 3 Continued

4. Journal entries for 2003

JOURNAL PAGE

	DATE	DESCRIPTION	POST REF.	DEBIT	CREDIT	
1						1
2						2
3						3
4						4
5						5
6						6
7						7
8						8
9						9
10						10
11						11
12						12
13						13
14						14
15						15
16						16
17						17
18						18
19						19
20						20
21						21
22						22
23						23
24						24
25						25
26						26
27						27
28						28
29						29
30						30
31						31
32						32

Name ____________________

Comp. Prob. 3 Continued

4. Concluded

JOURNAL

PAGE

	DATE		DESCRIPTION	POST REF.	DEBIT	CREDIT	
1							1
2							2
3							3
4							4
5							5
6							6
7							7
8							8
9							9
10							10
11							11
12							12
13							13
14							14
15							15
16							16
17							17
18							18
19							19
20							20
21							21
22							22
23							23
24							24
25							25
26							26
27							27
28							28
29							29
30							30
31							31
32							32

Comp. Prob. 3 Continued

5. Trial balance

Comp. Prob. 3 Continued

5. Concluded

6. Financial statements for 2003

Comp. Prob. 3 Continued

6. Concluded

P13-1 Transaction Analysis

1.–4.

5.

P13-2 Analysis of the Cash Account

1.

JOURNAL

PAGE

	DATE		DESCRIPTION	POST REF.	DEBIT	CREDIT	
1							1
2							2
3							3
4							4
5							5
6							6
7							7
8							8
9							9
10							10
11							11
12							12
13							13
14							14
15							15
16							16
17							17
18							18
19							19
20							20
21							21
22							22
23							23
24							24
25							25
26							26
27							27
28							28
29							29
30							30
31							31
32							32

Name ______________________________

P13-2 Concluded

2.

P13-3 Analyzing Cash Flows

1.–4.

JOURNAL PAGE

	DATE		DESCRIPTION	POST REF.	DEBIT	CREDIT	
1							1
2							2
3							3
4							4
5							5
6							6
7							7
8							8
9							9
10							10
11							11
12							12
13							13
14							14
15							15
16							16
17							17
18							18
19							19
20							20
21							21

5.

Name ______________________________

P13-6 Cash Flows from Operations (Indirect and Direct Methods)

1.

P13-6 Concluded

2.–3.

P13-7 Computation of Net Income from Cash Flows from Operations (Direct Method)

	Accrual Basis	Adjustments: Debits	Adjustments: Credits	Cash Basis

P13-8 Income Statement from Cash Flow Data

Name ______________________________

P13-9 Statement of Cash Flows (Indirect Method)

P13-10 Statement of Cash Flows (Direct Method)

1.–2.

Name ____________________

P13-10 Concluded

3.

P13-11 Statement of Cash Flows (Indirect Method)

1.

P13-11 Concluded

2.

P13-12 Unifying Concepts: Analysis of Operating, Investing, and Financing Activities

1.

P13-12 Concluded

2.